TEMPLES AND THE SPIRITUAL QUEST

SRIKANTH JOSHI

Copyright © Srikanth Joshi
All Rights Reserved.

This book has been published with all efforts taken to make the material error-free after the consent of the author. However, the author and the publisher do not assume and hereby disclaim any liability to any party for any loss, damage, or disruption caused by errors or omissions, whether such errors or omissions result from negligence, accident, or any other cause.

While every effort has been made to avoid any mistake or omission, this publication is being sold on the condition and understanding that neither the author nor the publishers or printers would be liable in any manner to any person by reason of any mistake or omission in this publication or for any action taken or omitted to be taken or advice rendered or accepted on the basis of this work. For any defect in printing or binding the publishers will be liable only to replace the defective copy by another copy of this work then available.

|| Om Shri Raghavendraya Namaha ||

This Book is dedicated to

my father Late Jois Govindachar

&

my little daughter Sriksha Joshi

Contents

Acknowledgements

I drew inspiration from my father, Late Jois Govindachar. He was a poet, dramatist and an actor.

My family has a lineage of scholars and writers who have contributed to the enrichment of Hari Dasa Sahitya and towards Kannada literature.

My School teachers have always motivated and inspired me to read and learn history, philosophy and literature. I am highly indebted to them.

Special Thanks to Sandeep Mukhami for his cover page photo and photos of Hampi.

Thanks to Sri Priyanka, my sister, who helped me in editing this book in her busy office schedule and family life.

This would not have been possible without the support of my colleagues, friends and all my family members.

The photos in the book are images purchased from Shutterstock.com and also from my friend Sandeep Mukhami with his consent.

Introduction

Trek to the snow-capped Kedarnath Temple, evening vedic chants at Chidambaram, solitude at Belur mutt, savoring temple cuisine at Udupi are some of the experiences that gave me a unique spiritual fulfillment. I felt, if we have the intention and focus towards these happenings, sync with these events, it gives us an enormous sense of joy above our paradigm of sensual pleasure.

The purpose of life is spirituality. Traveling to the ancient temples, pilgrimage, rare monuments and remote mystical places induces spiritual growth in us.

These journeys or visits are beyond our daily routine, to seek greater knowledge of self and supreme self. Our joy provides a deeper meaning and brings us a different perspective. India is the powerhouse of spirituality, and luckily I have been to many of these places; temples in lofty hills, snow-covered mountains, remote islands, high altitude stretches, coastal belts, moist places and historical wonders. There are moments I felt deeply connected to the almighty, cried, blown out of joy & ecstasy, hugged dear ones, experienced bliss of solitude. There were a plethora of emotions I have experienced.

I am bringing some of those unique places and moments for you all to relish and experience in this book. This is however, not a mere travelog, but feelings, deep expressions and historical connotations connected to these places. This covers places across India, and associated with different cultures and customs.

This is my sincere effort in enabling you to think & connect to some of the magnificent places in India. If you have lost in your mundane life, take time and experience these spiritual treasures, and unleash your imminent potential energy of joy and fulfillment.

> *"You have to grow inside out. None can teach you, None can make you spiritual, There is no other teacher but your own soul."*

- Swami Vivekananda

CHAPTER TWO

Udupi and Dharmasthala

"Oh Lord Krishna ! Did you feel your stay at Dwaraka and Mathura are boring ?

Is that the reason you came here near the beautiful coastal plains of Udupi ?"

My thoughts were similar to these lines from a Kannada devotional song after paying a visit to the famous shri krishna temple at Udupi.

Udupi, A popular coastal town of Karnataka, has many things to offer. Shri Krishna Temple of Udupi has unique features - One needs to take the darshana of the lord through nine small windows (Navagraha kindi). Some attribute this to *Nava randhra* of the body. This symbolizes that the abode of shri hari needs to be reached by crossing all the worldly things. Kadagola Krishna - Shri Krishna in a small form of a child folding a butter churner is a visual treat to both the eyes and the heart. There is childlike innocence on the face of the idol which cannot be forgotten.

Legends say this was the same Idol which devi Rukmini worshiped the lord in *Dwapara yuga*. When Shri Madhvacharya, the Philosophical Guru of *Madhwa shastra* rescued sailors on a ship near the shores of Malpe. He got a big piece of *gopichandana* from the people whom he saved as a token of respect and gift. Madhvacharya, with his *divya dristi* could identify the idol inside the gopichandana and established it in the Temple of Udupi. He also established eight mutts which we can see now near the mutt premises. We have the famous ChandraMouleshwara and Anantheshwara Temples also near the vicinity.

Photo Courtesy : Used under license from
shutterstock.com

Udupi stands for the cultural representation of the Tulu nadu (Southern Coastal Belt of Karnataka). I saw a representation of the culture in the form of architecture, customs, language and, not to forget, the famous Prasadam, which is a coastal cuisine of Karnataka. Having food here itself is a great experience and completes the visit in all respects. Beaches near Udupi are really nice as they are soaked in the bhakti along with the grandeur of nature. Vadabhandeshwara temple near the shores of Malpe has fascinating temple architecture depicting the typical coastal Karnataka style of construction. Shores of Malpe tell us different stories.

Not so far from Udupi lies the famous temple of Lord Manjunatha, which is the most famous temple in Karnataka. The ancient hamlet of Kuduma, which is known as Dharmasthala, stands for effluence of Dharma. Lord Manjunatha is the name of every household not only in Karnataka, but in neighboring states.

Lord Manjunatha signifies *Dharma* - even today, people take an oath in his name, and it is unbreachable. There are many unique aspects of this temple. This is the Shiva Temple worshiped as per the Vaishnava Traditions and the administration is maintained by local Jain chief points known as Dharmadhikari.

This is a place where many cultures meet and greet each other. Both the Vedic and Sramana (Jain) traditions are here to uphold the spirit of Dharma. Dharma does not mean religion or cult but the right path of living.

Udupi, Dharmasthala and many other places in the coastal belt of Karnataka portray the authentic legacy of customs and traditions continuously followed and preserved for more than a thousand years in Tulunadu. I got a flavor of local customs of Tulunadu engrossed with vedic customs, and they are inseparable here. Customs like *Bhuta kola* and Naga aradhana (Serpent worship) are very specific to this culture. All of these mirror an intrinsic sense of spirituality connected to the local people, customs, food varieties and language here.

Divinity is manifested in the form of nature here and the Western ghats are the witness for all of this play of god.

Photo Courtesy : *Used under license from shutterstock.com*

"*Lord Parusharama orders the sea to recede and give space next to the western ghats, and so this is called Parashurama kshetra. Later, serpents under the leadership of Vasuki converted the land for living , and so serpents are considered to be natural guardians of this land.*"

- Skanda Purana

CHAPTER THREE

Kedarnath

Photo Courtesy : Used under License from Shutterstock.com

Shiva, Adiyogi, stands at the pinnacle of yogic power and Kedarnath in the Himalayas is the symbol of *Sanatana Dharma*. Stood at nearly 3500 meters from sea level, it represents the ascension of the soul towards the almighty. I paid a visit to Kedanath in 2004 along with my family. I had an opportunity to trek to Kedarnath along with a group of devotees from Gaurikund to Kedarnath. This was my trek to remember and cherish.

There were different ways you could reach the Temple - by foot, mule, *palki* and even via helicopter to the base camp. I reached the Temple by the most exciting way, that is by foot. As you ascend the mountain, you will feel you are somehow ascending the higher steps of spirituality. Walking towards snow-capped mountains, within narrow lanes with streams of water nearby fills your heart with rejuvenating feelings. I felt I was a tiny particle in front of those majestic hills and peaks in a way philosophically representing self and almighty relationship. The Journey represents the journey of soul crossing difficult hindrances and samsara (worldly life with pain and temporary pleasures) to reach salvation. In a way, this trek symbolizes the metamorphosis of Realization or Moksha / Salvation.

As you reach the Temple point, you notice Nandi, the eternal vehicle of Lord Shiva waiting for his orders. The array of mountains behind the temple tells you all physical might are subservient to the Lord. Its worth taking a deep breath and meditating in the arena of the temple, and it is a lifetime experience. || Om Namah shivaya || resonates your soul and nourishes your fulfillment.

The pilgrimage is a prime part of Hindu rituals. There are few who take the path of renunciation of worldly duties and materialistic life, and give all their life to these practices. Many of us are not fortunate to take this path, but what we can definitely do is to absorb the spiritual vibes of these prime temples of Indian Tradition. Make the visit to these places special by knowing and understanding the significance through the scriptures and from learned men. If you get an opportunity to trek or walk to these places from a distance, do that as it adds to your spiritual saga in seeking god. Traveling up opens your heart for inner guidance. Connect to nature out there and sync your feelings with the aspects of serenial beauty present there. This is a belief we have in our ancient culture that doing these pilgrimages in the splendid nature gives us an enormous power and subtle happiness inside our heart. Belief is not just the norm here, but a practice to enrich ourselves. Hold onto your feelings that enrich yourself .

These practises of pilgrimage are mentioned in our ancient scriptures, and how even mighty kings and emperors in their time used to spend some part of their life here in the woods and mountains only to know how leading a life here makes them real emperors, and i.e to win over their sensual pleasures. These practises are present in parallel traditions of Buddhism and Jainism as well.

The importance of these visits is highlighted in many ancient Indian texts, including the Mahabharata. Teerth Yatra parva is a part of Vana Parva from Mahabharata which mentions and explains the importance of this. Bhagavatham mentions the significance while explaining the visit of Vidura to these places.

> "*sa nirgataḥ kaurava-puṇya-labdho*
> *gajāhvayāt tīrtha-padaḥ padāni*
> *anvākramat puṇya-cikīrṣayorvyām*
> *adhiṣṭhito yāni sahasra-mūrtiḥ*"

Bhagavatham (Sholka 3.1.17)

CHAPTER FOUR

Dakshineswar

Photo Courtesy : Used under license from
Shutterstock.com

Your list of visits to Indian temples will not be complete
unless you get the flavor of the eastern part of India in
general, and Bengal in particular. Dakshineswar, with the
abode of Maa Kali - Mother goddess, is the symbol of pure
love towards the universal mother. Bhavatarani is a form of
Kali worshiped in Bengal. Though this structure is only a
few centuries old, it has a history of being associated with

none other than Saint RamaKrishna Paramahamsa and his prime disciple, Swami Vivekananda. Located very close to the banks of the Hooghly River, the Temple structures have a magnetic force pulling with strings of the spiritual forces. It has a power to soak you in a sea of pure devotion towards the mother goddess.

I visited this temple very recently when I had to attend my classes at IIM Calcutta, and had a brief stint on my stay in Kolkata. I spent the most rejuvenating morning at Dakshineswar. Early morning ferry rides across the river with the Dakshineswar temple on one side, and Belur Mutt on the other are very graceful.

This Temple is built in the typical traditional Bengal School of Architecture with nine spine styles. This temple was founded by Rani Rashmoniji in 1855, a Philanthropist and an ardent devotee of Goddess Kali. The Aura of this place is still filled with innocent and pure love of devotion by Saint Ramakrishna Paramahansa towards the Goddess. RamaKrishna Paramahansa spent almost all of his life worshiping devi in this temple. His devotion with magnetic aura brought a disciple who later became - Swami Vivekanada, who established the Ramakrishna Mission.

Swami Vivekananda got inspiration in this place. He got a message from the divine force to fulfill his mission of spreading Sanatana Dharma. It is with this fame of spirituality at Dakshineswar that Swami Vivekananda became a torch bearer of the eternal Sanatana dharma, and the rest is history.

On the other side of the river there is Belur Mutt. It takes a ten minute ferry ride to reach there from Dakshinswar. It is the central place of Swami Ramakrishna Mission and all the activities started by Swami Vivekanada. This ferry ride takes you along the Hooghly river crossing

Vivekananda Sethu or bridge. As you take a ride, you feel you are getting deeply attached with this spiritual bonding of guru and his disciples. Bridge somehow personifies the bonding between the Guru and his disciple Swami Vivekananda. This resonates a feeling that Guru -Disciple bonding is stronger than these structures and is immortal.

I spent a couple of hours meditating and praying at this spot. It is the treasure of spirituality. Silence here speaks to you and heals all your sufferings. Whispers of Swami Ramakrishna Paramahansa are still heard by many here - " Ek baar Dakshineswar aao na". Whenever I think about this place and relish those memories , I feel like I hear " phir se Dakshineswar aao na" - Come to Dakshinswar again.

"All worship and spiritual discipline are directed to one end alone, namely, to get rid of worldly attachment. The more you meditate on God, the less you will be attached to the trifling things of the world"

Swami Ramakrishna Paramahamsa

Nava Brindavana

The Guru or the Teacher is given a very special place in Indian culture. He is someone who shows his disciples the path of knowledge and the path to salvation. The Madhwa school of thought (*Vedanta* school of philosophy) is one of the three prime schools of thought within the Vedanta framework of Indian Philosophy. I visited the sacred place of Nava*Brindavana*, which in itself stands as a testimony to this guru's lineage.

Across the side of the river from Hampi, a popular historical place in Karnataka, you find a small set of remote islands which are very close to a village known as Anegundi. Anegundi was the ancient town of Kishkinda noted in the Ramayana. You reach this place only via a small ferry ride, and there are no artificially constructed bridges along the river Tungabhadra.

I reached this place one fine early morning, and as you enter this island you will be mesmerized by the scenic portray with a small stream near the shores of this island, and crystal clear water and wonderful picturesque environment. I took a quick bath in the river and a few steps from the banks of the river you find the celestial place of the nine final resting places of the guru parampara - The Great Lineage of Gurus. There is no roof like structure for this and all of it is wide open, signifying the Vyaragya amsha i.e Virtue of dispassion shown by these saints.

Purandaradasa in his popular bhakti geete says "Guruvina gulamanaguva tanaka Doraiannada Mukuti" - which says without the grace of Guru one cannot reach the destiny of salvation.

All of these statements are brought to life in this place and are personified by the grace of the Guru. These saints are from different timelines, starting from the 14th till 17th century. Saint Vyasaraja - *Rajaguru* of VijayaNagar kingdom is the most prominent among the brindanavans. There is a historical connotation to why these saints decided that their final resting place would be near Anegundi. *Parikrama* or *Pradakshine* in this place gears up your spiritual essence and the experience cannot be explained in words.

There is a small Idol of Lord Hanuman - Bhima and Madhvacharya all in a single Idol symbolizing The Madwa order of worship towards the Lord Shri Hari.

"Prathamo Hanuman Namah - Dvitiyo Bhima evacha Poorna Pragna Tritiosthu Bhagvad karya sagatah"

In his first appearance as Hanuman in *Treta Yuga*, he served Shri Rama. In his second avatar as Bhimasena, in Dwapara, he carried out the orders of Shri Krishna. In his third avatar as Sriman Madhva (Poornapragna) he reiterated the voice of Shri Vyasadeva and became the greatest spiritual benefactor of mankind by preaching the Divine Teachings. There is an Idol of Lord Ranganatha as well here and completes your spiritual tour.

This is also popular as a mystic place, and many visitors are supposed to have experienced supernatural powers, which is a testimony from many local people there as well. Visiting this place fills you with the grace of the Guru.

"Anant Sansar Samudra Tar NaukayitabhyamGuru Bhaktidabhyam Vairagya Samrajyada Poojanabhyam Namo Namah Shri Shri Guru Padukabhyam"

-Adi Shankaracharya

Salutes to the sandals of my Guru, which is a boat which helps me,cross the endless ocean of life, which endows me, with the sense of devotion to my Guru, And by worship of which, I attain the status of renunciation.

"Rajadhani jayati saa gajagahvara sangnita - yatra bhanti gajaa madhwaradhantha dharanidharaha"

- Shri Vadiraja Teeratharu (Tirtha Prabhanda)

The City of Anegundi is phenomenal with the presence of the effluence of Madhwa saints.

CHAPTER SIX

Nubra Valley – Seat of Buddha

Photo Courtesy : Used under the license from shutterstock.com

A visit to Nubra Valley is one of the very special experiences. This lies in the paradise of Ladakh. The journey to Nubra valley from Leh passes via the world's famous Khardungla Pass and is a very adventurous one. Once you reach Nubra, you see a thirty three meter statue of Maitreya Buddha near the Dikshit Monastery facing down the Shyok river. Very near to that you have an area of sand dunes.

Prayer flags greet you at most places in Ladakh with good gestures and luck. Buddhist stupas at each and every corner of most of the towns there symbolize the culture of this geographical location.

I visited Ladakh in early April. It was still very cold, and I took a day or so to get acclimatized. With my interest in learning Buddhist schools of philosophy, I visited Dikshit monastery to understand the Vajrayana school of Buddhism. This is a school of Buddhism, which has additional tantric aspects along with *Mahayana* school of Buddhism.

Spirituality is a holistic feeling. There are always elements of aesthetics which motivate and increase motivation for life. Adventures can also be part of this path of spirituality when deeply imbibed with traditional values. There are elements of these adventures in Ladakh, which include going for a bike ride, some snow treks, and a double hump camel ride near sand dunes. Along with the monastery visit, this gave me a combo experience of spirituality.

Photo Courtesy : Used under the license from shutterstock.com

The super ingredient for this visit was the super sweet people there. The hospitality of these people is to be appreciated. People wishing us "Julley - Julley " pull us back to this place again.

I got a flavor of this culture with its intrinsic customs depicting a special way of living customized for high altitude. Simple living and meditation practices form the forefront of this culture.

Buddha stands for enlightenment, and his journey to find inner peace came with lot of teachings. He and his disciples spread those teachings across the globe. The vastness of those teachings and the diversity of those thoughts enriched with local details of living in Ladakh is what made this a special place to visit. Nubra Valley and Dikshit Monastery stand for the quintessence of spirituality.

Experience of the tranquility there and the chanting of the mantra || om mani padme hum || are the biggest take away.

CHAPTER SEVEN

Madurai Murugan

Photo Courtesy : Used under the license from
shutterstock.com

Muruga is another name for Lord Subramanya or
Kartikeya, who is a child of Lord Shiva. The form of
devotion and customs towards Lord Muruga is unique and
also spread across Tamilnadu. In my stint of several months
at Madurai, I relished and experienced, and got some

understanding of the bhakti cult at TamilNadu, which has been running across generations since the Sangam period. The Sangam era is an era of cultural epitome of Tamilnadu. Muruga and the culture of Tamilnadu cannot be separated. The essence of bhakti culture in TamilNadu is engrossed in devotion towards Lord Muruga in Tamil Nadu.

Thiruparankundram Temple is unique in nature with its temple having a cave-like structure. It does not have very tall *gopurams*, but the place unfolds inside the cave-like area with the sanctum sanctorium at the tail end of the cave. I could visualize the grandeur that would have been present at the peak of the Sangam period and Pandyan kingdom. There is a popular Tamil bhakti hymn - Skanda Shasti Kavacham, which emphasizes the bhakti towards Lord Subramanya (Son of Lord Shiva)

"Inthiran Mudala Yendisai Potra.Manthira Vadivel Varuga Varuga"

which means starting from Lord Indra, all the devatas of all eight directions come to Muruga to pay him their obeisances.

Manifestation of devotion towards Lord Muruga is presented in this Temple of "AruPadai Veedu" - Signifying the battlefield of Lord Muruga against Demons. Thiruparankundram is the first of the list, and there are five more places spread across different places of this south Indian state. Palani Murugan is another prominent among them.

People from almost all sections of communities are involved in the bhakti cult of Lord Murugan. As per the legend, Asuras (Rakshas) were to be defeated, and Lord Subramanya took the role of chief of the military - Deva

Senapati, and protected the good ones. The famous Thaipusam festival stands testimony for this cult, where a lot of things happen centered around this deity. I was astonished by the immense bhakti of the people, and saw people having their bodies pierced with the vel, which is the weapon symbol of Lord Muruga. People do this to get the grace of god, which is known as "Arul" in Tamil. Vel, or the weapon of the Lord, is given by his mother Parvathi to defeat the asuras. Philosophically, I metaphor that to bad karma and deeds, and with the grace of divinity, we will get rid of that through devotion.

The Culture of devotion at TamilNadu lies in a fact that it is deep-rooted and no amount of foreign forces and ideologies confronting the Sanatana Dharma could erase or reduce it. People practice local customs not just as an one-day affair but throughout their lives. My observations came true as I see a lot of people who have steadfast loyalty towards these traditions and, from time immemorial, the traditions are kept alive.

"Amarar   Idar   Theera   Amaram   Purintha Kumaranadi Nenjeh Kuri"

Dedication to Lord Kumaran who ended the problems of the Devas.We shall meditate on his lovely feet.
    - Skanda Sasti Kavacham

CHAPTER EIGHT

Chidambaram

The Concept of Cosmic Dance - Tandava is a divine dance performed by Shiva- Nataraja. It signifies the creation, preservation and dissolution cycle. The place and Temple at Chidambaram stands testimony for this concept of Sanatana Dharma.

Photo Courtesy : Used under license from
Shutterstock.com

Thillai Nataraja Temple is a temple situated very near to Mangrove (known as Pichavaram there) close to the east coast of India. The State of Consciousness, as the name signifies, would make you feel a unique spiritual platform associated with Lord Shiva. Unlike other Shaivite temples, there is no *Lingam* in this place and it is known as "Akasha Lingam", denoting the sky-space form of Lingam. This is attributed to the formlessness of God himself, as per some schools of vedic philosophies.

I spent a couple of days at this place, and I felt the feeling of the dance of divinity in a transcendental form. Every evening you spend here in the temple, with all the lights lit, and vedic recitals in the background, take your presence somewhere else, where the deity himself is performing the endless dance of ananda, which is an infinite state of happiness.

The architecture of the temple is majestic, and it is the biggest Shiva Temple in India. The temple also includes other deities, namely Lord Govindaraja (Vishnu in his reclining position) and Parvathi(Prasunambika Devi). The large area of the temple premises with many fascinating sculptures is a special addition to your visit.

Mystic Secret - Chidamabara Rahasya is an age-old concept and legend here. This message is conveyed here in a subtle form. I would interpret it as a soul-searching exercise to realize the almighty. Try to decipher your collection of musings here, and it gives a unfolding of a secret in itself. I strongly feel the divine force in his majestic Nataraja form is conveying the universal secret of which we the people or the human kind have got only a little so far. There is a lot to understand and realize from the form of Nataraja.

Photo Courtesy : Used under the license from
Shutterstock.com

Nataraja signifies the life force and the symbol of scientific theory. Many of the aspects from Indian traditions are closer to the understanding of modern day science. We need to appreciate the fact that our ancestors had a knack of expressing the elements of science through various symbols and customs. Chidambaram is the place where Science meets the traditions.

CHAPTER NINE

Hampi and Kashi

Varanasi is the living city of spiritualism. Hampi was the capital of the ancient kingdom of Vijayanagara. Both of these have made a greater impact.

Photo Courtesy : Used under the license from Shutterstock.com

Varanasi, Kashi or Banaras is the oldest living city in India and one among the oldest continuously inhabited in the world. The plethora of experiences felt at kashi cannot be explained or difficult to summarize in a single book. It has been motivating and guiding people who want to go in spiritual directions for not just centuries, but for thousands of years.It is not just the spiritual capital of India, but the entire world. It is the cradle of so many philosophies called Darshans in Indian philosophical terminology.

Kashi stands for the past, present, and the future as well. In contrast to many cities which are only known for their past, like Cairo in Egypt or Rome in Italy, unlike these places, the civilization here is not a piece in a museum but living practice and endorsement of all the customs running more than thousands of years. It is the fountainhead of spirituality.

I have visited Kashi once, but I am not satisfied with just one visit and the vastness of this place cannot be experienced in just a couple of days. Time you spend in the ghats near the river Ganga is a lifetime experience. Kashi stands for the Mukti, or salvation, and it is indeed true in a realistic sense, where you feel all the worldly things are not permanent. I am literally running out of words and expressions to capture the moments. For me, Kashi represents " the final journey of spirituality" and one fully soaked in it never comes back.

Hampi is one of the other places which drew much of my attention and focus. This is very close to my native place. I had an opportunity to visit this many times, and still feel there are many things to be covered and explored.

Photo Courtesy : Sandeep Mukhami

Like Kashi, Hampi is a very ancient city starting from the time of Ramayana till to the recent historical dates. It occupies a principal position in Indian culture and history. I saw here a living sense of nature and the amalgamation of time and life - streams of river flowing near to the town, troops of monkeys, wandering sadhus, ruins of ancient sculptures and monuments, living temples and festivities, ghats where people perform last rites and flocks of foreign travelers. Definitely, you get the miniscule flavor of Kashi here, and I personally felt that. It is known as "Dakshina Kashi" (Southern Kashi). It is a paradise for historians, adventurers,spiritual people and also for hippies. Again, like Kashi, it is difficult to cover the nitigrities of the experiences in a couple of pages. I am not going to the history and timeline of Hampi, but only to say that it adds a big set of experiences and all in the single zone of Hampi. Hampi is not just one single place, but feels like it is a big region providing a superset of emotions and musings for the travelers.

> *"Banaras is older than history, older than tradition, older even than legend, and looks twice as old as all of them put together."*

- Mark Twain

Photo Courtesy : Sandeep Mukhami

CHAPTER TEN

Wishful list never ends

India has so many places to visit, and for me it looks like the list will never end. This country has a great civilization, with which it has so many diversified customs and traditions which are spread across the length and breadth of the country. There are many of them which need to be explored and experienced. I feel there are different flavors of bhakti and cultural uniqueness in these places as well. The Essence of Sanatana Dharma is inherent in all these places , and only waiting for us to realize and relish. I have added some more of these places here to reflect upon based on my information and understanding.

Tiruvannamalai - Soul of Shiva

Arunachaleswara Temple is a famous temple in south India near the famous Arunachala Hill. The Hill is considered to be as Lingam itself or an iconic representation of Lord Shiva. Deity in the temple is attributed to the element fire among the pancha boothas (Five elements of nature). Sage Ramana Maharshi spent almost all his life preaching his teachings near this temple, and he is known for his teaching of "Self Enquiry". There are a lot of mystic saints still in this place.

Puri Jagannath - Ratha Yatra of Bhakti

The Famous temple of Puri Jagannath lies at the eastern coast of India. It is known for its *rath yatra* all over the world. It is said all the deities come to Puri to witness the Rath yatra when Lord Jagannath comes out of the temple along with his siblings Lord BalaBhadra and Subhadra. The Pantheon of gods celebrate and hail this event , and it is definitely mesmerizing for all of us to visit this temple and the festivities surrounding this place.

Dwarka and Somnath - Jewels of *Saurashtra*

Lord Krishna came to Dwarka and established this city. It belongs to him and all his devotees. Definitely not to miss this ancient place where the flute of Krishna still resonates in the hearts of the people. There is a mystic town submerged inside the deep waters of the sea next to the present town of Dwarka.

The list of Jyotirling starts from Somnath where Lord Som or Moon God did penance here and Jyotirling appeared. Unfortunately, this temple was destroyed many times by foreign invaders. They could destroy the structures here, but not the faith and essence of this. The Temple was reconstructed upholding the pride of this nation.

Pandharpur - Spiritual Walkathon

Jai Jai Vittala - Hari Hari Vittal Vittala. Panduranga is a favorite among millions of Kannada and Marathi households , and the inspiration for the Kannada and

Marathi bhakti cult. Innumerable devotional songs are composed in his name and enriched both Kannada and Marathi literature. Puranadara Dasa, Vijaya dasa, Sant Dhyaneswar, Sant Tukaram, Jagganatha Dasa, Sant Eknath and many more are attributed to the tradition of bhakti towards Pandharpur Vitthal.

"Pandarapura vemba dodda nagara , alli vithoba nemba dodda sahukara"

(Kannada devotional song - Dasara pada)

"Majhe Mahera Pandhari - Aahe Bheevre Chya Tiri"

(Marathi devotional song - Abhang)

Thousands of Devotees actually walk to this place every year, praying and singing the *keertanas* in Ashada month of the Hindu calendar to get a glimpse of Lord Vittal, and indeed, it is a walkathon of spirituality.

Harmandir Sahib - The Golden Temple

Wahe Guru ! Place of worship for all. Abode of God. Amritsar houses a magnificent golden temple symbolizing the golden ideals of Sikh Pant ! Millions of devotees visit this place and get vibes of Guru Grant Sahib - The Holy book of Sikh Pant.

In this spirit of realizing and finding the supreme self in every great thing we see, **the sacred search of the spiritual quest happens !**

"*ākāśāt patitaṃ toyaṃ yathāgacchati sāgaram .*
sarvadeva namaskāraḥ keśavaṃ prati gacchati"

- Vedic Hymn

As all raindrops falling from the sky reach the sea, so also the prayers to all divine aspects ultimately get to the Lord Keshava, who is the supreme ultimate reality.

"*yo māṃ paśhyati sarvatra sarvaṃ cha mayi paśhyati*
tasyāhaṃ na praṇaśhyāmi sa cha me na praṇaśhyati"

- Bhagavad Gita - 6.30

For those who find me everywhere and see all the things in me, I am never lost, nor are they ever lost to Me.

Photo Courtesy : Sandeep Mukhami

Glossary

- *Ashada - Is a month in the Hindu calendar that corresponds to June/July in the Gregorian calendar.*
- *Bhakti - Devotion*
- *Bhuta Kola - Form of Spirit worship*
- *Brindavana - Tower with holy basil ; used for the final resting place of saints who are buried.*
- *Dharma - the basic principle of divine law in Indian traditions; a code of proper conduct conforming to one's duty and nature*
- *Divya Drishti - Divine sight*
- *Dwapara Yuga - In Hinduism, It is the third of the four yugas (world ages) in a Yuga Cycle.*
- *Gopichandana - Sacred mud like material very special for all Vaishanavas*
- *Gopuram - A Large pyramidal tower over the entrance gate to a temple*
- *Jyotirling/ Lingam - A Jyotirlinga or Jyotirlingam, is a devotional representation of the Hindu god Shiva which are very prominent ; lingam represents to all other representation of shiva*
- *Madhwa Shastra - Philosophy given by Saint Madhwacharya*
- *Mahayana - School of Buddhism developed in India later to Theravada and is considered one of the two main existing branches of Buddhism*
- *Nava randhra - Openings in our body (Two eyes, two ears, your mouth, your nostrils, your anus and genitals)*
- *Palki- palanquin*
- *Parikrama/Pradakshine - (in Hinduism and Buddhism)*

the action or ritual of moving clockwise round an object of devotion as an indication of reverence.

- *Keertanas - Devotional song*
- *Rajaguru - Chief Guru for King*
- *Ramayana - Historical epic on Lord Rama glorifying his virtues*
- *Ratha Yatra - A ceremonial procession centered around a chariot carrying a holy image*
- *Sanatana Dharma - Eternal Dharma or the Hindu religion*
- *Saurastra - Is peninsular region of Gujarat in India*
- *Skanda Purana - Hindu texts glorifying the God. There are 18 and one among them is skanda purana*
- *Treta Yuga - In Hinduism, it is the second of the four yugas (world ages) in a Yuga Cycle.*
- *Vedanta - a Hindu philosophy based on the doctrine of the Upanishads in principle.*

www.ingramcontent.com/pod-product-compliance
Lightning Source LLC
Chambersburg PA
CBHW022121150726
47990CB00003B/1448